THE MILLENNIAL BIBLE

Direct Messages from Your Higher Self

THE
MILLENNIAL
BIBLE

Direct Messages from
Your Higher Self

ROBERT MARSHALL

LUMINARE PRESS
WWW.LUMINAREPRESS.COM

Printed in the United States of America

Cover Design: Claire Flint Last

Luminare Press
442 Charnelton St.
Eugene, OR 97401
www.luminarepress.com

LCCN: 2019913857
ISBN: 978-1-64388-206-2

I dedicate this book to my two guardian angels, Robert Sr. and Georgetta Marshall, who just happen to be incarnated in the flesh as my parents. Thank you for allowing me free rein to go out into the world and discover my own truth.

Contents

Acknowledgements

Mother, thank you for being my biggest supporter over the years. You have shown me the art of loving unconditionally. I am forever grateful to have experienced your love and truth in my life. I would also like to thank Empire of the Sun, Justice, Queen, Pink Floyd, Garbage, and Madonna. Your music served as a soundtrack to my ongoing healing while writing this book.

Introduction

The night belonged to the winter's chilling winds. Dogs barked excessively in the background as I stood at my side door in a daze of denial. I aimlessly scrolled through my phone, watching the supposed perfect lives of others. This daily activity of self-loathing only served as a distraction from myself and the painful present moment. I clung to my phone as if it had all the answers to my self-inflicted suffering.

I didn't see a single star, and the strong winds settled within my tired/overworked knees. Life seemed so hopeless and bleak, or so I thought to myself. I was looking to illusions and comparing myself to what I saw in the make-believe world of others online. I saw the past ten years of my life through the eyes of regret.

All my peers were married twice over or in high-paying careers, while I remained stuck in my childlike wonder. My need for escape was always present throughout my thirty-year life. I once perceived it as a gift and a good attribute to possess. However, in the "real world" it revealed itself as a crippling curse. I denied the greatest friend request I could have gotten, my intuitive voice.

I've had an on-and-off relationship with this intuitive voice. One minute I'd ask my higher self for guidance, and the next minute I'd doubt the synchronicities happening as a result of my prayers. With enough faith, action, and results, I've come to the realization that I have been wrong about everything. I never had to be the forgotten one or the person who allowed temporary circumstances to destroy his will. The sun had surely missed me, due to the dark cloud that adorned my negative aura.

I am writing these words to you while walking toward the edge of transformation. My friend, won't you join me? It is not my desire to be complacent, depressed, or defeated again. Is it yours? Today, my only wish is that you let these words nurture you in times of darkness. If you gain from reading my words, then you have done a great deed for my recovery. Our future selves will thank us greatly.

Many would think of the inner intuitive voice simply as brain chatter. However, I see things quite differently. This voice called out to me in the silence of that cold winter night. It let me know that I had an ally, and it never left my side. I let it guide me when writing these words in one of the darkest hours of my life.

So you see, my friend, you've never had to go at this alone. I hope you find a quiet space to read these direct messages. Within this silence is where the intuitive comrade waits patiently for a problem to solve. It is loyal, brutally honest, and wants the absolute best for you.

These direct messages were intuitively written to comfort my racing mind in times of poverty, victimhood, self-loathing, shame, fear, and heartbreak. These messages gave me the kick in the ass I needed. I'd like to think this inner intuitive voice led us to each other also. These words I write are a coming-of-age story for those who feel unseen by the world. This story is about our trials, tribulations, and triumphs throughout times of despair.

Within these pages are messages of great importance I wrote to myself, from a perspective of my higher self.

This book contains many narratives about how you and I became the master of our own destinies. It is a reflection of the feelings many millennials feel today, as we hide behind the flash of our smartphones. The message is simple: You are never truly alone in your despair. There is a friend within the depths of your mind, calling out to you. Will you answer the direct message from your higher self? I believe this is the greatest friend request you can ever receive. I hope you find comfort, abundance, strength, and pure love for yourself and others while reading this book. I want you to know there is much opportunity outside of your fears.

Millennials, you no longer have to be the "victim" or the "racists." We can choose to edge out a noble path for ourselves and leave our past traumas and programming to a cold deathbed. We can listen to the song that our soul whispers sweetly in our ear. Throughout these messages I hope you gain a deep sense of understanding for your suffering and the sufferings of others. Some topics are as follows:

- Depression
- Addiction
- Validation
- Poverty
- Sexual abuse in families
- Bigotry and victim-hood
- Our fear of people
- Sex fetishes
- Getting over massive heartbreak
- Rage
- The art of pretending for parental approval

Many of us are many different things for different people. I can attest to the fact that I am guilty of that. We ride on the ships of others in an ocean filled with an abundance of opportunities.

We may think of ourselves as feminists and portray a hero online. However, we blindly protect and obey our perverted fathers living across the hallway.

We may think because of our skin color that there is no way to get ahead in life. Furthermore, playing out this scenario of a victim and never finding true meaning in anything, because we are told so by parents.

We may think of ourselves as the dominant class and only associate with those of equal status. However, was it you who acquired the prestige or those before you like parents or grandparents?

For there is freedom outside of your suffering. You have an obligation to find truth and purpose in your own life. Drop the crutches you once balanced your false identities on. Choose to lean on the virtuous friend within the depths of your mind. This friend imprints narratives of encouragement, love, and acceptance upon our subconscious minds. Congratulations, you have one new friend request! Your best version is awaiting.

An Unseen Friend at the Edge of Demise

My friend,

You must hold out in this darkened forest of
terror. Perhaps trauma from many yesterdays
ago has kept you bewildered far too long.
Unable to let go, you married a demon dressed
in all black.
It digs its deceitful claws into your breathing
reality, leaving your tears diluted with loss.
Love has abandoned you at a cruel universal alter,
rendering your body vulnerable to the
upcoming feast and sacrifice.
Your annihilated body is hidden well among
the masses,
but your eyes reveal internal aching. It is a call
for help.
It is a call out for belonging. A love SOS sent
with the purest of intentions.
And still, you are never able to manifest this
sense of peace you have wanted for so long.

You refused vulnerability in that moment.
You chose to navigate through deformed vines
and blinding bushes,
with no sign of the dawning sun.
But still, you must hold out in this
darkened forest...

I once was the curious soul, such as yourself...
I hung onto that side door for many mornings,
with a cigarette in hand, entertaining my
darkest fears.
Like yours, it always burned out too quickly.
I would light up another one, as I flicked the butt
from the previous one.
It was representative to all the years
I felt were "lost."

I thought of every possible scenario to numb this
aching pain. However the knife was too dull,
and a single pill was much too weak.
The noose loosened, as I fell
onto the tipped over chair.
The guns would jam, as a single
tear adorned a once rosy cheek, which used
to rise with great optimism.

But still, I held out while my enchantment for
this dark forest disappeared.

For there is a friend, just at the
edge of your demise.

Robert Marshall

She will whisper belief into your right ear,
and hold your back steadily.
She will wrap you in her gentleness,
while you practice patience with an
eager spirit.
She will reveal a reality to you,
that was buried within your soul.
For, this is why you must hold out...
For there is a friend just at the
edge of your demise.

Hold out, my friend.

LONELINESS:

We Are Not an Island

Dear Friend,

I saw your eyes open with resistance this morning. The sound of garbage trucks, dogs barking, and vengeful winds pierced your thin windows. This house is not a home, but was it ever? No pictures rest on the walls, and the clocks are all wrong. The silence is loud, and your heart is void. Do you ache in abandonment and fear? I once did and was made to feel ashamed of this mysterious pain, which tugged at my heart. I buried it within the muddy grave of my subconscious mind. Later, it manifested itself in an outpouring of lack, fear, and the need to control.

Does your heart silently whisper to your subconscious while you sleep? Do you take the time to hear its request? I've felt tides of true love rise to my throat, as you've experienced through the night. However, we awaken terrified of the one thing we desire the most. This attitude has left both me and you aloof, finding refuge in wrinkled sheets. Our pillows stay warm from our quivering bodies, unable to find comforting heat. Have you grown to desire a loyal shadow to walk beside yours?

I once was an island like you. I was surrounded by the fears of my mind, only to find out that life passed me by.

I saw love, water, and serenity in my passing dreams but refused to block out the receding tides of lack. I didn't have enough faith to trust that the water would always come back to shore. Like you, I've felt the disconnection, resentment, and fear that comes with long periods of isolation.

We are not an island, but the surroundings that beautify its sacred grounds. Life is the sun that kissed you by the shore and the moonlight, which stole your heart. It isn't the feeling of emptiness you felt upon rising today. Life isn't the heartbreak, letdowns, and betrayals you hold onto. Let them go in peace, and know that something better will arrive in divine order.

Life isn't the corporation, which you dread working for. Execute a plan to leave your life-draining duties at once. Life is the peace you felt at the edge of that island surrounded by shooting stars. The feeling of gratitude arises whenever you take the time out to observe this truth. Begin to pull in the sun while balancing the full moon on your shoulders. Can you feel the tide begin to come back again? The water purifies the soles of your feet and tickles your ankles. This is life, and this is where you can begin to dream again. You're never alone and neither was I. Today, I want you to begin to take advantage of all that surrounds you, and use it as a tool.

Use that feeling of isolation to better understand yourself. By embracing the silence of creation, you can begin to create a new life. You no longer have to marvel from afar on this island of your mind. You now have a life with like-minded friends, colleagues, and a lover. I know you will create someone who will love you beyond all measure. Create a partner in your mind, who will effortlessly find their way home in your darkest hour. Create the career that brings you to tears whenever you think about it. Lend your ear in the moments when your racing mind needs it the most. This loneliness can be transmuted into success, self-mastery, and true love, which is undying.

Today I declare to your tired eyes that I will never leave your side. You were never truly alone, because I am the lender of wings to tired spirits. My only request is that you use this gift to soar and explore the depths of your heart. Find out who you are and what your direct needs may be. You are the architect of the greatest love story yet to be told. A warm embrace awaits you, followed by kisses that bring peace to your aching body. Bring your eyes beyond the cracked blinds, and step outside. Outside of this abandoned and quiet home is where love awaits you. It is true, heavenly, intoxicating, and omnipresent. I've gifted you my wings; now fly. We are not an island.

1. Practice visualization that brings forth strong emotion. Begin to feel love enter your life. Listen to your favorite love song while driving. Take yourself out to that popular restaurant. Dress your best, because you are enough tonight!

2. Begin to seek out like-minded groups of people with whom to share your inner world. Your chances of finding someone are slim if you stay closed off from the world. Remember, we are not an island.

3. Make the most of your alone time instead of entertaining the idea of loneliness. Take up a new hobby, join a fitness club, take a course, etc.

4. Know that love is yours now. This isn't about deserving or being worthy. Love is my birthright. Believe this truth, and watch how the world begins to open up for you. Hold yourself in spirit and embrace this vulnerability.

Lulling the Inner Beast to Sleep

Dear Friend,

Today I stand with you in the midst of pure and utter chaos. Take a few seconds to look around at the destruction before us. Does this place look familiar to you? Dark clouds adorn the skies, and rain has begun to fall from your eyes. This dilapidated city is where you once were so comfortable in your addiction. This city serves as the battleground for the fight of your life. It is you versus your addictions! The roads are uneven, and the skyscrapers are leaning sideways. Together we watch them fall before us, further damaging the cracked roadways. Addiction has left nothing in this city (your mind) the same. I wander beside you as we mourn what once was a beautiful place.

The skyscrapers represent your relationships. Darkened clouds have formed upon these massive structures you have built on sand. Our urges could hardly go ignored, making it easy for the addiction beast to ravage our bodies and minds. We stood docile among dimmed phone screens, entranced at a fantasy. We drank from the poison of society and got drunk. We have penetrated the fleshly veils of Mother Nature. We feed the monster within, as it prepares for fire and brimstone upon our frail bodies. A beautiful wreck we are—among this once sacred city.

I beg of you to realize that these shackles are not real. This addiction is nothing more than an invisible barrier. However, what does exist is that childhood smile before the morning sun. It was a symbol of innocence before the abuse to your body began. You needed nothing because you had everything inside of you. The afternoon sun basked in your presence as you explored life inside of a pure mind. You showed gratitude toward the day and expected miracles always. What happened to the child that smiled before the morning sun? Surely, you haven't forgotten the smile, which brought up the sun and lowered the moon. We must find this great wonder again within this city.

The ugly beast plucks his head aside the dilapidated buildings. His body is mutilated and covered with open wounds. This beast reeks of regrets and bitterness. Do not fear, because I will be standing beside you throughout this battle. I declare, this beast will no longer be the ruining of your relationships. So smile under this full moon, and bring about the morning sun. Allow your inner-will to create your heart's desire. You no longer need to dwell in past mistakes or tragedies. Your only true escape is inside of creation. It doesn't reside in a man, woman, drink, or any substance. Your truth is inside of that fiery heart, which must slay the beast.

Are you ready for war, my friend? Begin to face this inner beast with courage and strength. Know that any fear is just an illusion that blinds you from victory. Smile at that morning sun, and bask in its possibilities. Freedom lies in your ability to be able to create from within. Meaningless addiction is no match for that sacred space of tranquility and wonder you had as a child.

Let us restore this once-broken city within you. Together we will create a dwelling of bliss. Together we will rebuild what once was broken. Watch out for fiery horns and wings falling before us, as the beast accepts his defeat. We have already won this predetermined war from within. The beast's yellow eyes blend into the gray of night. Sun arises from that smile of yours. You heart is full of gratitude for the coming morning. Night is gone, and eternity is spent within the warm rays of possibility once again. You have won, and your mind has been transformed once again. Was their ever anything to fear? Could this beast have been an inner illusion of the fears we cradle within undeveloped arms?

The need to escape was never greater than the need to create. These addictions only lulled our dreams to sleep, serving as a Band-Aid. Desire seeps out of these cracked grounds, giving way to our roots. Begin now to sow seeds of faith, gratitude, wealth, happiness, and true love. Riches will arise as quickly as you brought up the sun. I believe in you and so should you! Together we have lulled this beast to sleep, making way for a better city within you.

1. Remember how happy you were as a kid? Try to recapture that feeling again. Dedication is required, and things won't be easy. Spend some time reflecting and the answers will come.

2. Temporary pleasure is often followed by feelings of uncertainty. It's not all about the finish line, but the journey is much more satisfying. It is certainly filled with setbacks for you to navigate. This isn't a race, so be patient, but never stop moving toward your worthy ideal.

3. Listen to your inner spirit, and try to understand what it is saying to your flesh. Do these desires align with the spirits? Will these urges further or ruin your relationships?

4. Find your purpose by exploring that child-like wonder. Creating is a true high and supersedes any alcohol, drug, person, place, or thing. This I know to be true, my friend!

5. Be patient, loving, forgiving, and nurturing to yourself. Remember, the sun always rises and so can you. You have a power within to shift, bend, and break anything in your life by uprooting. Get your shovel and began to dig up everything you have hidden from others!

Robert Marshall

HOW TO LET GO:

Staring Back at the World

Dear Friend,

I see through your momentary happiness, as we ride on the rings of Saturn. The sun sees great pain in your eyes as you've driven alone for a thousand miles. This road has been full of rough patches and long stretches of isolation. It hurts, doesn't it? There is a tightness in your chest, and your heart has broken once again. You think back on how it went wrong and the part you played. Has this left you unable to focus on the infinite ahead? You've worried yourself sick about things you can't control.

Has the past grabbed your attention once again? You stare through this cosmic rearview with heavy eyes and a tightened grip on the rocket's steering wheel. Why do you wonder and marvel at such a tragic past? Have you grown addicted to the hurt? Does it bind you on this rocky road we travel together? I beg of you to look at the wonder that lies before you and me. The planets shine brightly for you within this spectacle of glittered darkness.

A crystallized future awaits us as shooting stars pass our front window. But yet, you still hold on to this idea of who you once were. Be gentle with yourself, and know that mistakes happen. Find peace to forgive yourself and others.

Implant new community within a pure and driven mind until you find your tribe. Focus on the road ahead, and look out into the mind of the universe.

Galaxies await you and me. They will teach us about the power of faith. Faith will bring you the new circumstances you desire. You will love again with an openness you never shared before. You will begin to see your wounds healed, as you let them go with peace. You will show gratitude at all the endless possibility that lies in front of you. You're a beautiful cosmic vessel that has the capability to bring life into you. At this moment begin to focus on the road ahead. Look out into the wonder in front of us.

Diamonds rain from above as we drive along mystical grounds. We no longer desire to marvel at passing asteroids and a world that rocked our core. Instead, let us show gratitude toward the possibility of a fantastical destiny awaiting patiently. Let the planetary energies find refuge in your mind to express their will. Grab ahold of the love energy and let it express itself through you. Do the will of compassion, and show gratitude for all the painful lessons learned. Without them you wouldn't have been able to realize the heart's desire.

Do the will of forgiving, and watch the shackles fall from your body. Drive on, my friend, because you've got billions of stars awaiting your smile. You pull the planets in with your magnetic aura. The universe surrounds you in awe, recognizing you as its perfect manifestation. Vibrant colors arise along with the thought of a bright future for you. This destiny awaits you with open arms and provides us with purpose.

Bid your past farewell with love and gratitude. Begin to shift your focus back toward the wondrous road ahead.

Begin to dream again, and watch how the planets respond to you. We are free to travel as far as we desire. There is nothing holding us back, not even this vehicle. You are free and with freedom comes great responsibility. Steer clear of any disbelief that you cannot have this beauty that awaits you and I. Avoid distractions from tailgaters that lurk in the rearview. They only ride close behind to distract you from paradise ahead. Once we arrive at the destination, you will find other partners to ride beside you throughout space. You'll no longer be bothered by what's in your rearview mirror. Continue to travel this road and always stay curious.

You are free from the shackles of regret, and heaven reflects its light in your wide eyes. You are once again aligned with the virgin-like spark of curiosity. Lay your past down on the universal field, and watch it diminish before your eyes. I've got a good feeling about you. Remember, what isn't in front of you can never deter you. Ride on, my friend, ride on.

1. It is not easy to forgive, but you must in order to reach this personal paradise you hold within. Let the person, situation, or thing go with love and appreciation. Begin to look forward to more wondrous miracles that can take place in your life.

2. Imagine the future you desire for yourself and what brings you peace and meaning. Let these feelings outweigh the pains of the past. Keep telling yourself that things happened for a reason, and good awaits you. You are not made up wholly of these heartbreaking experiences. You don't have to wear the suit of regret and guilt anymore.

3. There is never a lack of love, goodness, and truth to go around. What you once thought was good may in fact be a much lesser version of what awaits you.

4. Be patient with yourself if any negative thoughts arise. Follow the divine order of life, and adorn your spirit with trinkets of empathy. Understand that each person has their own path to follow. There will be many who go off-road and take detours away from you. Let them travel without you. What is yours will stay along for the ride.

5. On this road to self-discovery remember to create boundaries. Abandon your past hurt and gift your sub-conscious with images of a balanced life. Create your perfect destination within your mind and meditate on it day and night.

SOCIAL ANXIETY:

Defeating the Reaper's Dark Orchestra

Friend,

I see that today was like many days you had once before. Happiness has escaped you quicker than it has arrived. Raindrops awakened you, and the skies are grim once again. Hazy smoke intertwines with darkened storm clouds. The floors squeak like your aching bones as your feet touch cold hardwood floors.

You've awakened tired and depleted from nocturnal storms in your bedroom. A strong hand with its black glove squeezes at your racing heart. You begin to wonder how you measure up to the masses awaiting outside fate's door. You try to loosen its firm grip and struggle to look at this aggressor in the eye. However, you feel its evil gaze locked on you. Music begins to play outside, and you are pulled through this prison that is home.

I saw your limp body dragged from those ravaged sheets. You tried to lessen the anxiety within your chest with a temporary escape through your unfinished beer. You grabbed the drink left over from the previous sunset to ease your nerves. I thought we already conquered the beast within your inner city? Is it cold inside from the fear that has stiffened your bones? Your head is forced to the door, but you can never face the masses. You peer with shameful eyes out the crack of your front door. The grim reaper laughs sadistically behind your hunched back as you gasp for air.

His voice is stern, cold, and uninviting. He whispers words of destruction in your receptive ear. Can't you see what he is doing to you? He is force-feeding you anxiety and fear on a plate of shame. You've eaten with him before, unaware that his cravings are not yours. Why are you so scared of being seen?

His nails begin to pierce the skin on the back of your neck. This isn't a home but rather a fortress you hide away in. Fear reflects from your eyes as these once-solid walls come crashing down around you. You stand front and center with death at your doorstep. You feel powerless as he smashes your head into the door with a killer's intent once more.

Your front door of protection swings open as you face his orchestra of darkness. The orchestra begin to play notes, which resonate with your sabotaging thoughts. You try to close the door, but it is ripped off of its hinges. Your face is bloodied, and your body is weakened under his spell. This massive orchestra plays on each and every insecurity hidden within your flesh. Their lifeless bodies sway in unison, as the reaper leads them into a familiar melody. Their slanted eyes begin to blacken while their faces remain expressionless and pale. Black capes adorn their fragile skeleton-like bodies.

The violinist plays a twisted fiddle, which makes your palms sweat. Her brittle hands will play notes of despair to your ears. You remain froze in confusion as horns, trumpets, and flutes join in for your melodic demise. This song is all too familiar, and it has eroded your confidence. Your heart begins to beat out of your chest. You feel seen and unseen at the same time. Your palms absorb heat, and beads of sweat form on your nose.

Friend, I beg of you to cover your ears during this illusionary orchestra of fear. The notes that they play are in no relation to your true self. There is a song that has resided in your heart since childhood. This is a beautifully crafted song about courage, faith, and self-love. This song once played over and over inside a mind that looked to the day with enthusiasm. Do you not realize that you are the composer? You have the ability within you to create a beautiful symphony. Reject the masses at your door that perform songs of doubt before you. Block out this noise that was orchestrated for your destruction.

So smash the violin of fear by showing compassion for yourself. Fear is only an instrument used to deter you from the heart's calling. Begin to strum beautiful notes embodying your greatest version. Destroy these barbwire strings from the harp instrument, which was used to create the shame you feel. Hold your heart delicately, as you silence its rapid beating from the judgmental crowd.

Remember that the song within you is a masterpiece that needs total expression outwardly. So leave your lust down at this open door, and focus on your cleansing. There is a brighter future ahead of you, which fear has no role in.

His grasp will surely loosen as you begin to practice self-love. The reaper will be repelled from your inner light and descend back to the night. Allow the glow from heaven to eliminate the darkness at your doorstep. You are the master composer of the greatest love song ever written. This song consists of gratitude, courage, and faith to move forward despite worries. Play the song that you've been afraid to perform in front of the world. The masses await your truth. Most importantly, your heart and soul await your awakening. By awakening you finally accept yourself and others. These dark harmonic frequencies can no longer make you feel inferior. Play your song, and create a beautiful soundtrack to a life of virtue.

1. No one is perfect, especially the people who condemn your very existence. We are all trying to navigate through the uncertainty that is life. Remember this in times where you feel less than.

2. The biggest competition we face often is with ourselves and the present day. What will you do to make sure you win today?

3. Adding productive habits is a definite way to increase self-worth. Eliminating toxic addictions and replacing them with a greater purpose is the goal. This will give you the strength to face the world with an unfazed vigor.

4. Just as your fears have a voice, so does your courage. Focus on what it is that you want to sing on the stage of life. Feel empowered, free, and valued at this very moment. Sing your truth!

5. Hold yourself with a sense of respect when you venture into society. Feel yourself inside of your body, and look at the outside world as a stimulating experience. Begin to search out things, places, and people that resonate with your inner song. Every singer needs a band!

THE RACE:

Comparing Yourself
with Others

My friend,

I sense that your belief is skewed and fearful. Did you know happiness begins at your mark on this arena turf? Instead you believe this perceived happiness begins at the finish line. Why do you look at the path ahead as dreadful? This path is full of insights, challenges, and lessons to learn. The hurdles you perceive as rejections are only bonuses in the race of life.

Each hurdle you leap over ensures a valuable treasure. Has your perception of success leaned upon the thoughts of others? Has your intuition been silenced in fear of appearing different from your spectators? Your wants and needs could never perfectly align with society's. Your victories are to be had only in the space of true intimacy. This isn't about anyone else, and there is no need to sprint with shame under your heels. Hold your head high in this marathon, and let strong winds motivate you. These strong winds will push you forward when times seem grim.

There is a single star in the sky that will illuminate the spirit. It shines brightly unto you as spectators watch from the stands. However, it is important to drown out the noise of the crowd. You've cared far too much about the opinions of spectators. Allow this arena of judgment to burn all around you.

Prepare for self-realization and transformation as the retractable roof opens on this stadium arena. Let the fires out through opening your mind to all thoughts of gratitude. When doing so, you are granted the chance to listen to your heart's desire. It will never lead you astray as long as you silence out the masses violently yelling before you.

You've run for so long with a tight chest and short breaths. Smoke has engulfed your lungs and made you think twice about running another lap. I beg of you to see the challenges ahead as strength points. Every setback is merely a prelude to your soul's desire. Surely you wouldn't let a small failure tire your anxious feet?

If you must walk, then walk in the name of faith. If you choose to run, then I encourage you to run toward purpose and responsibility. For there is no other competition on this field but you and only you. The lights are shining brightly as you begin to put one foot in front of the other. Your fatigue will be in direct correlation with your thoughts. Do not be bogged down with limiting beliefs and the success of others. This is a marathon solely meant to teach you patience, gratitude, and self-knowledge. So today, drown out your perceived competition and spectators in this game called life. There is so much to run for, my weary friend. On your mark, get set, and go!

1. This isn't about anyone else but you. There is no need to rush life. Stay on track, and success will not allude you.

2. Drown out the noise of societal pressures and opinions of family, friends, and peers. No one can tell your story quite like you can. Let others have their opinions and be unfazed by them. Remember, no one else can author the book to your life. Take charge, and press forward with your goals despite how big they are. You have an inspiring story that must be told!

3. There are valuable treasures that come from perceived setbacks. Never feel embarrassed about failures or things not going as planned for you. It's simply an early chapter in the long story of a wondrous life. Look forward to the hurdles when running at life.

4. Take time to tune out social media and direct that attention to yourself. Often, we can become depressed by simply viewing others who appear more successful in life. It's time to focus on you and not this false image you've attached to yourself.

5. Show acts of gratitude to others who have what you desire. There is no need to be anxious, bitter, or jealous. Surely if they can do it, then so can you. There is no shortage of money, success, and happiness on this earth. There will be few who are willing to help you but many who are not.

How Loving Yourself Helped You Climb Mountains

Dear Friend,

We have travelled throughout different dimensions inside your creative mind. Thus far you have destroyed internal monsters that waged war on your soul. You have basked in the marvels of the planetary energies. You have even managed to silence a dark orchestra consisting of negative thoughts. However, there is still an anchor on your cold heart.

I sense that you've been misused and abused emotionally. Has your trust gone south with your once-beating heart? Are you tired of giving your peace away? You exchange your time and energy in exchange for instant gratification. It brings me great pain to know that you give so freely to everyone but yourself. Why do you deny your soul intimacy and seek it first in others?

You have this belief that you are a nice guy/girl. However, I see things much differently than your physical eye does. Your treasure lies on top of a mountain you built for others. The love you gave everyone all sits 33,000 feet above sea level. It is a mountaintop that everyone benefitted from but you. They got to see the best views from atop this mountain at your expense.

Its peak overlooks the Atlantic Ocean into sparkling waters below. You reached to the heavens for help but they left you broken and lost. Being alone has been your greatest fear thus far, which is why you choose to be "nice." Your faith in society has gone south as your friends dance so freely. As a result, you have nothing left to spare in this time of misery. Where are the ones who you invested so much time and energy into? They have all abandoned you and took your virtues for granted.

Rise off your back and begin to look toward the heavens. Standing before us is a monument that must be explored by you and only you. In its cracks and creases lies great wisdom, unbeknownst to you. Do not let your knees be weakened by rising altitudes, which bring cold weather. As you climb, trust yourself and your abilities to reach the top.

Do not be angry at what you have created. Be grateful for the power to manifest something so awe-inspiring. By the sweat of your brow you created a beautiful monument. So why is it that you still feel powerless and empty? Friends, ex-lovers, and family are not to blame for your fear. It is only you standing before this mountain, and you have every right to go forward. As you plant your feet to take the first step, remember to imprint the soil with faith. Dig your fingertips into these rocks, assuring your grip is strong. A sense of confidence will overcome you as you climb higher.

Joyfully gaze at the beauty that lies before your eyes. This mountain is covered in purple quartz. Speckles of neon green and sunset orange also sparkle effortlessly from the mountain. We are overlooking crashing waves from a mystic blue ocean of opportunity. As you climb farther to the top, be cautious of falling debris. These passing rocks only represent your fears falling into the waters. They will fall to the bottom of the ocean, giving you the freedom to explore your soul. With bloodied hands and callous palms you are determined beyond measure. Your intentions have been made clear to the heavens. The treasure is your freedom, which lies ahead. A beautiful ray of light awaits your presence as you climb farther to the top.

This climb has taught you everything you needed to know about yourself. It has taught you acceptance, forgiveness, and compassion for others. It has also taught you the value in self-love. It was you who stood alone and made the first leap. It was you who mustered the courage to continue the route, despite falling debris.

New experiences are within reach of your mangled hands. Grab onto this treasure, and lift yourself up from the ledge. Now pull yourself together and stand at attention. Look out into the world, and marvel at what surrounds you. The sun rose for you and so did your consciousness. You are now fully capable of appreciating the climb you took alone. A sense of contentment, peace, and strength will come over you as a result. You realize this climb was only about learning to value oneself. The treasure still remained atop of paradise and was never stolen by others. It awaited your arrival despite the thieves who tried to steal its essence.

So I say this to you today: create many mountains. Each mountain serves as a soul challenge for your advancement. Explore the surrounding terrains and valleys of your soul. Stand in gratitude and acceptance at the challenges that wait within each mountain you conquer. Although they stand tall, they are no match for your inner strength. You can be the creator or destroyer of all that is within your reality. It was you all along and no one else. Stand amidst this beautiful scenery, and hold yourself tightly. You will learn the secrets to your life at the high altitudes of these mountains. Look out into the world with a relentless vigor. Beautiful and blissful pastures sit before you. However, you wouldn't have known this if you never climbed. Life is filled with beautiful climbs that show us the strength lying dormant inside. So embrace the climb and bask in the accomplishment of self-mastery.

1. Refuse to let heartbreaks and betrayals detour you from your goals. You had a mission before you met them. Continue on where you left off before you became love drunk or hungry for attention.

2. Look to each challenge you face as a chance to "level up." Great lessons often come in the form of a setback or failure. Have the courage to move forward, and know that you will become stronger from each lesson.

3. Cultivate the good in you and work from that source. It is much easier to navigate from a place of peace versus a place of torment and chaos.

4. Your past experiences can show you many things about yourself. Learn from these traumas, and extract empathy for others from them. To forgive ourselves is to forgive others also.

Frozen on the Stimuli Island

My lustful friend,

Was the heat unbearable between your dampened bed sheets? You rose out of bed with a confidence, once hidden in previous battles. I know just how silent those abandoned nights can be. There is a longing within your pelvis to feel another's warmth while tracing skin with your lips and fingertips. Instead, you escape once more to Stimuli Island, a fictitious land that serves as breeding ground for your sex cravings. This is a place where you've felt safe since the cravings began. You've hidden away under the sheets, peering out only to see what stimulates your sexual senses. But what about the things that make your soul vibrate? What about heart arousal and all that is gifted to you from this act?

Your hidden desire has always been connection, and you know it! You've admitted your falsehoods and fetishes to yourself, yet your deepest "need" scares you. This "need" is imperative and will reunite you with the heart space. Its warmth is reminiscent of a summer day, as your innocent smile outshined the sun. The morning sun would be no match for your inner light back then. You found joy in the day and struggled to keep your gratitude within the body. Unknowingly, you were a walking mantra and performed divination on a daily basis. Connection was a pleasure in the afternoons and you found it effortless in your childhood to be vulnerable with others.

You expressed your needs to the best of your abilities, and they were met with a warm embrace and assurance. This was an assurance that held true to the words it whispered. My decree is that you will never have to ache, long, or crave another.

What you desire is a love that is pure like your mother's, yet you sabotage your own efforts regularly. Could it be that we are unknowingly in a battle for our very essence? Does the pain shoot up your stomach when you plant your feet to get out of bed? Does the feeling of not having anyone pierce through your chest? I once was unable to face the day and immediately looked toward a release, as you do so often. My eyes would open to a reality that I didn't want to participate in. I would travel to this Island of Stimuli like you've done so many times.

I thought I was escaping by giving myself unearned pleasure. In reality, all I did was hide myself from the world. We both know there is a distinct difference between the act of escaping and hiding. Escaping is energetically embracing your heart's desires as real while leaving the old behind. Hiding is being ignorant to the fact that an escape exists. You've failed daily in your attempts to hide because I see you clearly. You've sat hunched over with your face covered from the world for too long.

We've become entranced within an artificial light of instant gratification. However, our greatest distraction will serve as an ever-present reminder. This reminder is that we need each other, and it has never been more apparent. Do not fret; at the edge of this island is where you will find personal freedom. I have faced many battles like this, and looked toward the adversaries with an uncertainty in my gut, not sure how I could conquer this addiction. Our lust has stranded us into an island of isolation and depression. Our bed has floated on treacherous waters, and we've failed to send out a smoke signal to heaven.

Scrolling through endless waves of temporary satisfaction, we find ourselves addicted to the dopamine hit. Our beds—once a place of rest and imagination—have now become unbearable. Instead, we've found a release in these illusions of love. We have become a voyeur to the fantasies we so desperately want to express with another. Your bed is a reminder of all the things you wished for that haven't manifested yet.

Now we sit in the middle of a grey ocean polluted with desperation. The waters have become aggressive and move swiftly toward shore. They take shape of every lustful thought that you've held onto, rising one hundred feet above shore. Does this imagery look familiar to you? Do these aggressive waves of forming waters scare you?

Qtesh (the goddess of lust) owns where our feet are currently planted. You've awakened on this day and finally opened your eyes. You are beginning to realize the world that surrounded this lonely bed you float on. This island is cold, and the skies are dark and thick. Venus shines above us with no moon or sun in sight. She pours her seduction down upon our orgasmic bodies and belts out sounds of pleasure. This Venus energy rains down upon us, further deepening our feet into this quicksand of illusion. It blinds us, making one vulnerable to the thought patterns of lust she emits. These thoughts consist of entitlement, shame, and addiction.

Naked bodies of gods and goddesses sway among the darkened skies. They caress their perfectly sculpted bodies as you watch from below. Entranced, you watch with eyes full of pleasure and submission. Legs, arms, breasts, chests, arches, and smooth necks engulf your vision. A soft breath followed by a subtle kiss touches your neck. However, you fear to look them in the eye, due to their gigantic and intimidating statures. Does this scenario remind you of the fear you feel when among the masses? Do you feel like people can sense you are hiding something dark and perverted?

You passively disregard the love that could be yours due to your feeling of unworthiness. Do not lower your eyes to love in public and later seek it in your comfort zone. In this "comfort zone" there is no place for companionship, breakthroughs, and new beginnings.

I will continue to hold your sweaty palms, but only you can break this illusion. These giant deities are nothing more than your hidden expressions and truths. They lie underneath your lust, waiting to be nurtured by a real companion. Let faith take precedence and know that you, too, deserve a helping hand. You don't have to always go at the outside world alone.

What you need is a partner whose grip is everlasting in your palms. These steady hands will assure you and run their fingers through your hair. These faithful hands long to be in yours, never losing their firm grip. Give up your lust and your need to fulfill all your "needs" alone. There is a soul that is here to walk beside you, unthreatening to your independence.

Robert Marshall

So let the false gods and goddesses fall to their knees without praise. They will kneel and be weakened by your retentive nature, no longer capable of draining you dry. Faith and goodwill is with you at enemy lines.

Let the lust energy die and release it from your consciousness. Turn the blue light of your phone down, because you've outgrown the voyeuristic tendencies of perverts before you. You no longer crave orgasms followed by nothingness. You are no longer peeping through the peephole to love and life. You are now going after the dark skies that adorn this tragic island. You are dedicated, motivated, and determined to paint colors across them instead of your sacred secretion.

You are no longer sensitive to the touch of loneliness. Instead, the soul sings a beautiful song of clarity, wisdom, and freedom. So stand at the feet of your needs in submission and with a pure heart. There is nothing to justify, my friend. Turn the blue light of your phone down, my friend.

1. Begin to pinpoint what triggers this feeling of loneliness. Is it your living space, failed relationships, etc.? Do you often feel the need to release after feeling these negative emotions? Awareness is always the greatest step on the ladder of self-realization.

2. Change up your idle time in exchange for reading, self-reflection, and enhancing any existing relationships. If you can't dive in head-first, at least dip your toe in the water.

3. What needs are you hiding that you feel cannot be met? What is it that you need to experience with another? Maybe you really value intimacy instead of this lust. This could come in the form of a soul-fulfilling conversation where someone listens to your secrets. Or, it could be a willing spirit that you can be vulnerable with, without the fear of judgment.

4. Life should never be lived through the peephole. You are more than a spectator to the love, passion, and animalistic heat that you desire to experience with someone else. Know and trust that someone out there has the capability to satisfy your deepest desires. There is no need to envy, lust, or become stimulated by illusions of others. What you want is here now, and it is up to you to bring it to life.

"I Once Was a Monster"

My fire-breathing friend,
This message should extinguish the wildfires within your neglected heart. With frozen emotional valves, I was missing the touch of another. I smashed trust, punched through bridges, and left past lovers trembling in fear at the sound of my voice. I once was a monster too! I sense that past trauma has had an extended stay in your lungs, making it harder to breathe. Has your trust gone to the abyss of a darkened soul, never to raise its head above waters again? Once more, this familiar roar has shattered a thousand mirrors you refuse to face. They revealed everything that you considered ugly, untrue, and fleeting about yourself.

I once was a monster like you. You've held onto Satan's horn too long, waiting for a savior from this rage you feel. However, your angels are far too wise for these tactics of deception you display. They know where the cement door to the underground tunnel lies. Beyond that cement door is a child desperately trying to drown out a city that ignored them. This city could be your friends, family, past loves, or associates. Does this inner rage come from feeling invisible, unheard, and forgotten? You screamed at the top of your lungs as the masses trampled over your cries from above.

THE MILLENNIAL BIBLE   53

You've began to see red again, and the bull charges ahead at the matador's request.

The more you cried out, the more the masses continued to drown you out. Your belligerence and bitterness do not hold enough power to push this tunnel door open. Your fire could never free you totally because it is rooted in negativity. I once was a monster like you too!

I wallowed in self-pity and was controlled by my bitterness. I pushed and pushed until I was the last left in a war that never truly existed. Divinity, love, and society left me to my anger, only to find myself becoming more aloof. I beg of you to cut these toxic cords from your shaking body! Leave your unbridled rage in the depths of that cold city sewer.

Refrain from charging like a bull when it sees red. Instead, battle that inner-rage with a sense of tenderness. Confine those bitter thoughts to the underground cell of your mind. Promptly make a decision to escape this misery you feel. Thoughts of love, healing, and forgiveness can never be suppressed. Use each of these virtues to free yourself from this underground purgatory. You will soon find that this door will begin to open, allowing your light to shine out. By releasing what is good into the world, you can begin to experience this from others in your reality.

Feeling unseen and unheard will then be a thing of the past. You will be a walking manifestation of all things good and true.

Looking back, you will begin to ponder how you could have stayed underground for so long. Your body once housed a darkness that could stiffen the bravest spine. Housed in rage you once were but no more! You once were angry at the flick of a flame, but no more. You once were a monster, but that monster is no more.

Robert Marshall

1. Ask yourself: "Why do I respond to things the way I do?" Perhaps it's not about anyone but you. Ask yourself those hard questions about the life you are living and where you may be feeling unfulfilled.

2. Check your environment and begin to assess if it's a healthy one for you. This could be a toxic work situation or neighborhood you live in. Feelings of entrapment can always leave us feeling angered. So today, make the decision to free yourself from things that aren't congruent to your essence.

3. To forgive someone is like throwing a boomerang of compassion out into the universe. If you're struggling with this concept, know that things take time. Ultimately by forgiving yourself you can forgive others as well. No one is perfect and maybe one day you'll need that same understanding that you gave out.

4. People are attracted to things that shine. Therefore, begin today to put your "best self" out into society. Know that we have all suffered and it is of great importance that you set a better example for yourself and others. By doing this you will become a source instead of a consumer. Let your cup overflow with gratitude and the thrill that comes from just being alive!

5. Remember that anger is a prelude to loss. Loss of friends, family, and lovers. Refrain from anger, and watch how your story changes.

6. Watch your anger from the perspective of the inflicted. See how terrifying it is for another to witness that much

darkness inside a single person. See the holes in the wall, and hear the loud roars coming from your mouth. Surely this will give you clarity on how others may feel as a result of this rage you hold inside.

"Shattering the Castle Door of Compulsive Habits"

You were shattered like the screen you stare into. No longer pleading, longing, or following your heart's direction. You've subconsciously navigated into stagnation and away from your personal bliss. Your heart lies dormant inside of the box you've placed at this astral door, which resembles a castle. You're surrounded by the presumed grandeur of others, which makes you complacent. Its interior is dark but smooth while offering you a peephole from within its confines. Your heart lies within the box in submission to your voyeuristic tendencies. However, you've distracted yourself from these enclosing velvet walls. The closing walls only compress their will onto your blissful ignorance.

You were shattered like the screen you stare into. You've built kingdoms from your insecurities. You are nestled comfortably in between thorns and roses surrounding this castle. You've poured time and attention into its 5D green pastures that sway so seductively under a warm spring sun. You look to it with envy, jealousy, and a lustful curiosity. Why won't you just live your life, instead of watching others? Begin to pour your love into the surrounding grass and sand under the moon's healing. Allow the sun to do its job in the waking morning. Find your courage to do, be, and embody whatever it is you desire. My friend, your truth lies between your gut and heart. It longs to travel through you and express itself from the tongue. Instead, you remain frozen from fear, facing this massive door you've created from within.

This box containing your heart sits at the castle door, resting under its massive mahogany exterior. This door represents all that you fear. It serves as a barrier between who society wants you to be and who you truly are. Why do you feel so intimidated at its massive structure? Is it because this door shows you your hidden greatness through its iron embellishments surrounding the border? You sit in submission, refusing to walk through its massive exterior. Instead, you stand at this doorstep paralyzed in fear, with a gifted box containing all that you are. Why won't you just live, instead of living through others?

Do your dreams and desires bring fear upon your body? Has your creative eye been poisoned by the opinion of the dark knights behind you on this land? They only seek to control your emotions and you ignorantly give it to them by peering outside of self. These are the ones who lack the sun of summer mornings. The fearful will always grieve in the illuminating nights of mother moon, only to manifest their deepest fears. This light is fake and fleeting.

The creativity they once had was destroyed by many false moons, eclipsing their free will. They play it safe like you've begun to do. However, that fateful moment has come to where you must choose. Will you open this door, or will you join those who wait behind you? This castle's door is bursting at its core. Love, health, and wealth are seeping out under its sandy-stone foundation. Know that it's just a door and nothing more. Un-gift your heart, and pick it up from this doorstep.

Your courage will rise as you begin to break this door down. However, your attempts are not desperate or one of urgency. Instead they are rooted in knowledge of self and your strong will. Each hacking will be methodic and swift in its movement. Why won't you just live and be? Break the door down!

1. Don't wait for others to move until you take control of your life. The story of your life has no other main star. It is filled with many beautiful people, but ultimately it is you who has the control over circumstances.

2. No matter what social media tells you, not everyone has it together and even if they did, it is none of your business. Focus on yourself and creating a noble existence.

3. Eliminate jealous patterns you feel about people you perceive to be better than you. Instead, congratulate them in your mind and wish them more success. Negative emotions only sabotage your divinity and halt the process of your life's work.

4. Treat your goals with urgency, as if they were a child trapped in a burning home. Let fear represent the door between you and your dreams. By kicking this door down you rescue not only your dreams, but yourself.

5. Distractions are nothing more than patterns set in play subconsciously to keep you away from any perceived danger. That danger can represent your enormous dreams, which you think can't possibly come true. I'm here to tell your that this presumption is dead wrong. Began to find comfort in the risk involved to combat these distractions, one act at a time. It could be something simple, such as taking an hour out to write down goals. Your dreams may be scary but they are far from unrealistic or impossible.

Robert Marshall

SEXUAL FETISHES:

Fetishes and Their Origins

My friend,

Many years ago I felt so free when in her arms. We played for hours on the back of the dawning fall, acting as if summer could last forever. She looked so beautiful and brought my heart to a comforting rhythm. We both were kids and couldn't understand why we were drawn to each other. Her name was Gracie, and she had angelic hands that healed my tired feet.

I was blissfully ignorant to the changing seasons and their dolefulness. Gracie and I resisted autumn, and wrestled with Mother Nature's ever-changing tendencies to separate two individuals. Leaves would fall, revealing their mortality to my pumpkin-shaped face. All was simple, and love wasn't a concept that I could comprehend just yet. It just flowed, effortlessly finding its way through her gentle hands upon my tired little feet. I was just a boy who adored being cared for after a playful summer day by my best friend. I would run through her door with eager toes patiently waiting for my dear Gracie to relieve my aching feet with her hands. That small neighborhood was the entire world to me back then.

I never knew there were new lands to explore outside of that block. However, one could've assumed I had walked thousands of miles by the pungent smell in the air. I'd leave my shoes at Gracie's door and greet her mother with my usual muddy embrace. She was sweet, never turning me away despite preoccupations with her own untraveled roads in life. Her daughter was my first love, unknowingly.

Gracie's mother's nose turned upward, as she pondered how a boy could run graveled roads all afternoon. I needed no rest but only her accepting hands. Through her then-thirteen-year-old hands, I became dependent on fairy tales. I believed there would be hands to always heal my aching feet when tired.

Years passed, and we both travelled further apart. Although we were in the same neighborhood, both life and age began its tale of trickery. I travelled away from home as I grew of age. In reality, it was nothing more than fate pulling our lives in different directions. We sacrificed ourselves by stretching our arms while trying to hold our deteriorating bond. I was stuck in lust while the rest of the world was falling in love.

Many miles were lost in the midst of seeking out pleasure, which was really a yearning for my once childhood love. However, no embrace was as true as my healer's hands. There was no warmth in the touch of my lovers after her. Like yours, my confidence had dissipated onto crinkled motel sheets and kisses with eyes wide open. It meant nothing to me, and surely I was nothing to them. I was simply a passing whisper, which tickled the fancy in their pelvises. I whored myself out to the beast within my belly, allowing parasites to feed on my lust. I inhaled my lovers' scents through the soles of their hands and feet but still thought of Gracie. I thrusted deeper and deeper inside my victim, hoping to find meaning.

I carried the neglect from Gracie in the bedroom and out into the world. It stained relationships and stripped me of my confidence. My head hung low, looking for the perfect set of toes or healing hands, which heightened my arousal. So I ask you tonight, what is it that you crave and tremble for? Has this secret fetish taken over all your senses, leaving your better judgment to a weakened will?

IS IT A WARM MOUTH YOU CRAVE, TO GENTLY KISS ALL the memories of past lovers goodbye? Maybe it is a shapely backside that arches at your command? You use this fetish as a wheel to roll over the past you kept buried for so long. What is it that gets the tingle ignited within your pelvis? My uncontrollable cravings left me a shell of my former self. I was unable to defend myself against my fetishes. I was still a boy looking for a trusted ear like my beloved Gracie's. My feet bled on the adjacent roads of self-loathing and denial.

I sought out body parts familiar to my sensations of a happy time in life. I spun atop of a heightened tail while tickling my nose in wet flesh. I was unaware that these bodies were so much more than a "get off." They were souls just like me, and I was ignorant to their individual suffering. I only looked to get my fix from their vulnerable limbs, feasting on their scented breasts, moist lips, and soft thighs.

I was just a boy missing the love he once felt after playing all day with his best friend. I was searching, wanting, and desperately needing to be taken care of. I was lost, but knew I couldn't go back to Gracie's. I fell in lust, while the rest of the world was falling in love, including Gracie. I wasn't the one who she choose, as we hadn't spoken in years.

I beg of you to mend your disconnections and heal your broken home. Extract love from these memories, and leave your trauma to the losses of the past. Walk away knowing that nothing could be perfect. There is a space for reconstruction amongst the devastation your past thoughts may bring. The lessons you learned set the foundation for a new dwelling within reach.

This new home is somewhere to express your deepest desires. Surrender your tired feet at a side door, and you'll never have to search again. There will be hands to heal you and a familiar warmth to wrap your body in. Come as your broken self, and begin to let a new love expression reignite you.

Tonight belongs to you and your desires. Meet your needs under the eclipse, and wait for a gift. Fill your home with remembrance of love, compassion, and tenderness. Express your desires to eager ears that await your presence. This is home, and you are loved madly, deeply, and beyond physical life.

1. Consider your fetish as a cry for help. What help do you need after pondering on this theory in silence? How can you express this even deeper need for help to a partner or potential one?

2. We all have things that we admire and are attracted to. There is nothing to be ashamed of. Instead of running away, embrace your fetish. Try to figure out where it came from and begin to trace back to your first impressions of love and intimacy.

3. Remember that people are not items. Therefore, create a healthy balance in your relationships while still meeting your needs. Your partner or future partner is much more than a body part. Worship all of them and appreciate their presence in your life.

4. One big drawback to our strong sexual urges is a lack of self-discipline. Remember, it's all about balance and not living inside a lustful mind all day. Use that fiery heat you feel about your fetish and apply it to mastering this realm of life. You will be surprised what you can accomplish when transmuting your horniness upwards toward that brain of yours.

GETTING OVER AN EX:

"Oh No, Let Thou Go"

OH NO NOT AGAIN, I SENSE YOU ARE ENTRANCED BY PAST memories. You purposely prolong your firm grip on a broken heart. Oh no, you must let thou go! Your ex is just a feather in a hurricane within this experience. Gently and forgivingly, you must let them go. Why must you treat them as if they are the hurricane? You've let them knock down the towers you took years building. They recklessly pillaged the pastures within your mind. Now all that remains is brown grass and deserted skies.

Oh no not again! I sense you still hold allegiance to your exes wishy-washy nature. You purified yourself in false light, only to be killed slowly from within. You never saw it coming but the deception had slowly spread throughout. Oh no, you must let thou go! Purify your heart within the dry heat of let-downs and release their toxicity. Let it seep out your pores and unto the bedroom floor. Wipe yourself clean and repeat the process until they flee from your mind.

Oh no not again! I sense they are in your dreams? You carry the good memories with you throughout each painful morning. Oh no, you must let thou go! The bad outweighed the temporary good, and this union never cracked the spring soil. The flowers did not bloom, and they had no intention on growing with you. You were only a feather within their hurricane of an experience. However, unlike you they know this because they were the deceiver. Their life is still well intact after shattering your heart. In fact, their towers are much more beautiful due to the destruction of yours. But still, you must let thou go! Forgive the deceit, understand the lies, and heal from holidays and birthdays they ghosted you on.

Oh no not again, you must let them flee. Awaken from the slumber you remained in since your ex departed. They never were the one for you, but only one to point you in the right direction. Now you realize what it is that you want and disdain what you don't. Now you truly know what love should feel, taste, smell, and look like.

Oh yes, I sense that you are finally letting them go. You are preparing for a storm consisting of velvet roses amongst butter-cup clouds. Your feather has transformed into a set of angel wings, saving you from the dreadful fall. The wind could no longer carry you on its own. A love savior descended upon the skies to swoop in on your limp body.

They didn't save you, but instead they showed you the beauty that rested under you. Oh yes, there is a place where your love is validated and reciprocated! Oh no, there is no room in your new relationship for toxic memories! Your feather has been restored and is ready for a safe landing.

There are plenty of blooming pastures to explore on your way to love. Let this journey pull you inward and embrace uncertainty. Know that where you land is exactly where you are meant to be. There is a love much better for you, and in time you will surely know this empathetically. For this is why you must let them go.

1. The term "letting go" should not be in relation to suppressing painful experiences. It's totally normal to have painful feelings, which come from cheating or a mutual break-up. It's better to feel those feelings now and allow yourself the time to heal. Releasing is the key when it comes to toxic relationships.

2. Go into the "intuitive sauna" of your mind and seek out silence. Whatever thoughts come to your mind, allow them no energy and do not fight them. Instead, let the dry sauna walls of your mind heat up the body and shed your baggage. Sweat your ex out of the system daily if you have to.

3. Know your worth and what it is that you need from another. Set boundaries, and hold a healthy respect for yourself. Get to know yourself by doing things like exercise, solo dates, and trips out of town alone. You deserve respect, consideration, appreciation, and devotion. Cultivate these things from within by standing up to the world alone for once. By taking this action, you will look next to you one day, and be surprised someone is standing beside you in admiration. Then you will know that love has never left you. It only has transformed into its ultimate expression.

4. Ask yourself, do you really desire someone who is inconsistent with you? Hold your red flags high whenever you feel you are being taken for granted. Wave them to the skies, and let your decree be one of understanding followed by immediate release of the person.

5. It may take a short time, or it may take a long time. Either way you must continue moving forward while affirming to yourself that day will break once you become filled with light. Keep applying pressure to your goals in life. Your heightened action will serve as the catalysts for the change you seek in relationships. You can and will get through this no matter what!

PARENTAL OPPRESSION, PART 1:

"Under Azalea's Hijab"

Friend,

Today I sense that you are pretending. Allow me to tell you a story about someone just like you. Her name was Azalea, and she pretended to be free, just like you. There was great potential beyond her brown eyes. She was unable to breathe under a heavy hijab, or so she thought. She rolled over in bed next to a perfect stranger for far too many seasons, unable to look at herself due to her pretending. Her friends were really free while she just pretended to be. She was in mourning over a life that was a creation of her traditions and elders. A life of normalcy was never hers, and she felt it deeply every time she was around her obedient mother. She craved to be absorbed into a pot of self-expression one day. She was missing the only friend she had yet to meet (herself).

Under this hijab lies expression in a glass bottle, stuck amongst quicksand in a windstorm. Day by day she fled away to that special place inside her mind. She stirred her curiosity with a golden spoon and feasted on the coming of her freedom. She was more than a loyal daughter. She was more than a strict religion. She was more than what others wanted her to be. She was a young woman, ready to take her life into that windstorm she faced behind glass.

She hoped to pursue fame and fortune. She would dance to the beat of her own drum while kissing strangers under neon lights. She would grace the red carpets with an essence unmatched. She would take a liking to all that glittered in gold. The covers of magazines were adorned by her beauty, and all of Hollywood would fall to their knees.

There was so much potential beyond those brown eyes of Azalea. Her father knew this secret and only tightened her glass bottle. It was so hard for Azalea to breathe. Her dreams would be no match for the rage he displayed. Her father's dreams would be intertwined with her predetermined fate. He weighted the already heavy family load with strict expectations of his only prize possession (Azalea).

Under this hijab was a mind focused on escaping tyranny. She rolled through fancy destinations of self-discovery. In her travels she found a love to call her own. He kissed her heart-shaped lips with his darkened, velvet fleshed pillows of lips. She met friends that were different than the ones back home. She married a hippie who resembled Jimmy Hendrix. The two made love amongst a backdrop of redemption. She now knew a truth that was buried by her father's firm hands. The world he desperately tried to hide from her was full of beautiful contrast. She saw rainbows in the eyes of strangers while walking on golden stars.

Life wasn't to be lived inside the confines of his rulership. Daddy's house could not contain her giant beating heart, which splattered color amongst his holy walls. Now she knew whose love was conditional versus unconditional. Now she knew just who and what she had to become.

Azalea was more than a mute daughter confined to her controller's hip. She was magic in a bottle, the chill in the windstorm, and the creator of her own life. If only she could wake up and plan this great escape in her reality. But she remains in quicksand, trapped in her glass bottle, as the unforgiving wind passes through her obedient heart. She will forever be a good little girl, and experience life through the eyes of her fathers.

1. A time will come when you feel you have no friends or family due to your life decisions. These decisions can be your career, political /religious views, love life, or sexual orientation. Remember, your greatest friend is within you, and you have the power to push ahead. When all others flee, there is an unseen force that will guide your precious heart toward better relationships.

2. Your happiness should not be sacrificed for your parent's approval. Not giving a damn is a fun trait to develop in growing up. Allow yourself at least three "I don't give a damn" moments each year. Of course, when you are practicing this act you should already be living alone.

3. Find local support groups, and get involved in a field of interest. This will lessen the pain you feel from being disowned by your peers, family, or friends. Journaling also helps when done consistently.

4. If your family and friends give you a healthy platform to express yourself, disregard the first three notes. It is much better to express your feelings and not harbor animosity toward overbearing relationships. However, if no compromises can be made, then you must remove yourself.

5. Set the example in your family or community. Be the living proof that dreams can come true. Break all paradigms that do not correspond to the essence within you. You have the power to be a living miracle on earth. Be practical, and welcome any rejection that

may come from this. Others will secretly admire from afar as you do the supposed impossible by breaking away from toxic relationships and parents.

MASCULINE INTENT:

Healing the Crucified Western Man

My brother,

Tonight calloused hands must become soft to the touch.
Let your iron triggers unwed from those brittle fingers. You
have grown into a victimized cactus. The areoles and spines
of boredom engulf our dormancy, crippling productivity. I
sense you have confined your truth to a small darkened
space. You are hidden, like the secrets you withhold from
the world. Society has covered your bloodied body in mis-
information and outrageous expectation. They punish you
for not being bulletproof among Lucifer's firing squad.

Tonight calloused hands must become soft to the touch.
Leave your superhero cape at the open door. Dive into
the intuitive flow of your inner truth, and disregard flimsy
arrows headed toward your skull. Have you missed magnetic hands and equal transfers of affection? Do you ache
for the feel of wind-kissed glaciers upon the stubble on
your neck? Goosebumps arise as you've come to find that
only you can save yourself.

Tonight calloused hands must become soft to the touch.
A father will surely fail once, but you must learn from his

mistakes. A mother's touch can become hardened from the expectations of the world. However, you must learn from her pain. A brother or sister may lack the ability to lead by example or protect you. However, you must never lay your bloodied swords down if clean.

Tonight calloused hands must become soft to the touch. Let spirit into your war-ridden exterior. Allow its tenderness to seep into your alleged "thick skin." Burn a candle beside your tear-stained window. Hold yourself gently, like a mother with a newborn baby. Assure yourself in the face of uncertainty, like a father would with a defeated boy. Lay your swords down at bedside only if they are bloody from combat. You will then realize that you are a worthy participant in this battle for greatness. You are now an active participant in the world you've often shunned.

Tonight calloused hands must become soft to the touch. Man is taught to hunt for everything, except for his authentic self. It calls out to him through testosterone-filled rants consisting of Googled opinions about his supposed unworthiness. It is a cry within a well-disguised roar. This supposed masculinity you display overshadows the life you've secretly longed for. As a result you have become The Great Pretender. It is this pretender who steals glances at the moon while maintaining a poker face. He is the supposed alpha male who preys on the broken, further advancing him in this psychotic game of deceit.

Tonight calloused hands must become soft to the touch. Is your cup no longer filled with possibility, leaving your dry mouth unquenched? My brother, let the truth exit your body and upgrade your senses. Walk on the runway of vulnerability as the world snaps pictures in awe of your masculine frame. Take each step with head high and shoulders back, and know your "safe place" is within. You will never have to be the great pretender in your safe place. It is here where you will find courage in vulnerability.

On this night, calloused hands became soft to the touch. On this night you are respected and seen as the thunder in catastrophic storms. We will bleed as one and find our strength together on this path of illusions. We will leave our lust at the gates of our personal hells, and chase nothing but our dreams. Along the way if we stumble we will swiftly adapt to the cards dealt. This will be the recipe for a fantastical life and true masculinity.

We will take back what we spilled upon folded napkins. We will live a life that is mystical but unapologetically bold when faced with oppression of our truth. I am your assuring rain, cleansing any thoughts of self-doubt you may be feeling right now. I am the calming breeze, echoing encouraging words into your anxious mind.

Tonight calloused hands must become soft to the touch. So let the battle for your soul began. It will serve as a prelude to the war that society has waged on you. Many will be surprised to see that you no longer need armor, and the swords were much too heavy to remain logged within. Lay your body out for the cleansing, and expand your broad chest to the moon. Tonight calloused hands must become soft to the touch.

There is a mystical man within us who represents balance, tranquility, love, and strength. He has no need to size up potential threats, because his feet are firmly engraved in truth. The crooked expectations of society are no match for his stoic stature. Find this man and integrate him into your reality. At that moment you will know what it truly means to be a man. Tonight, calloused hands were embraced by an angel.

Soft to the touch…

1. People often seek to control through opinions. The best way to guard your essence from this is by staying present in the moment. If you listen long enough you can easily spot their fears, insecurities, and perceptions of themselves. Let other people's projections be just that—projections. Never allow the thoughts, beliefs, and opinions of the masses to turn you into a victim.

2. You have the right to be vulnerable and intimate with yourself. This includes plenty of alone-time, meditation, or whatever form of relaxation you practice. We give so much of our time and precious lifeforce to things outside of us, with no return in investment. Tonight, let's find a purpose and pursue that instead. There are many battles to be had, so let's join in on this challenging game of self-mastery.

3. You deserve the love you subconsciously seek through others. But first, we must go back to those times were we felt powerless. We must learn to face these triggers head-on. All the things we swept under the bed of life must come up for cleansing. It will never be trendy for a man to suppress his authenticity. We must crave more responsibility in this world. Responsibility, truth, and overcoming adversity are our birthrights.

4. Express yourself through adopting worthwhile hobbies, and move forward in those new interests. It is perfectly normal to have interest outside of women and sex. Maybe just one of these new hobbies can turn into a love. Take that even further, and imagine doing that thing you love

as a career. You may just end up meeting a love in doing what you love. See where I'm going with this?

5. If no one else can, hold yourself tonight. Assure yourself like a concerned lover would, when facing self-doubt, lack of self-esteem, and any other self-defeating beliefs. Embrace your skin with your calloused hands. Tell yourself that it is OK to get lost when en route to a better life. This only shows we are taking risks without the security of a happy ending. Keep trying and pressing forward while staying flexible about your outcome.

OVERCOMING POVERTY:

"You Never Were a Victim"

My troubled friend,

Do cold Midwest winters and violent summers make it hard for your spirit to breathe? You have been stuck in this reality, birthed in poverty with no forewarning of how hard life can get. Bullets light up the sky like your smile did many summers ago. Present day brings the lighting of half a cigarette to the sound of belligerent winds. That damn cigarette always stays broken in half. Synthetic highs have become an escape to the enchanted life you wish to find. Your treasure is just beyond these city slums.

Spring brings hope while autumn dries out your plan to escape the ghetto. You ride the weakened back of hope and sending scientific prayers to a deaf sky. Prolific dreams were often pierced by missiles under many blood moons. This ill-fated self-narration outweighed miracles to come. Your optimism plummeted to a bullet-riddled concrete. Has the alcohol become an escape to the enchanted life you once wished to find? My friend, our treasure is just beyond the city slums.

There are two palms that will thrust themselves into your lower back. They are the hands that will gently guide you to your heart's song. Standing above you are musical notes of peace in the sky, while your hands wave hello to the sun. I will say this with the utmost certainty—there is a way out for you, my dear friend. There is a synchronistic song guiding you to the riches in life. Anger, violence, and poverty will be a thing of the past for you.

Today, dreams of a well-rounded life are standing before you. You are more than your trappings, ethnicity, or what the world declares you as. The red robin has delivered a message to your distracted mind. Take this as a divine message from spirit. It swirls within the starved gut of where you hide your great potential.

Go ahead and cry a little, but let it be from sweet relief. Pour your gratitude amongst the kindred spirits who may be stuck how you once were. Reach back and do for friends who cannot do for themselves just yet. There is enchantment beyond your suffering, poverty, and sense of abandonment. For there is a new life awaiting just beyond these war-ridden streets. Poverty has never been a friend, but only a challenging teacher.

Let your inner eye buzz while envisioning the enchanted life you see for yourself. Sun-kissed boy, you were never really trapped. You were never a victim to circumstance or the oppressive boot. You have everything you ever needed. The enchanted life awaits us, so leave your victimhood behind. Lay down your feelings of unworthiness. The enchanted life awaits us, my friend.

NOTES TO SELF:

1. Start envisioning the life you want for yourself. What's your ending scene look like? Make your vision strong and continue to build on it within the mind. Get specific and be creative with the lifestyle you wish to obtain. What does your car, house, and spouse look like? What type of music is playing from the balcony of your waterfront home?

2. There is always a way out for those living in poverty. Disciplined people have an innate ability to rise above obscurity, despite their upbringings. It is of utmost importance that you not be affected by environmental matters. Ignore petty confrontations and avoid places, people, and things that reinforce what you perceive as your trapping.

3. A virtuous life will surely flee from your grasp when accepting fear as real. Silencing your soul's song will repel potential manifestations from coming to past. This is only temporary!

4. You don't owe anything to the place where you come from. A limitless spirit is what you are. Go shake the concrete up amongst this beautiful plane of existence. A wise man never limits his potential to his current reality or a specific place he lived, especially if the present reality or place was not adding value to his or her life.

"Penelope, I Believe in You"

TRAGEDY IS A TALE OF YOUNG FOOLS SUBMITTING TO THE wills of their controller. Penelope is happily ignorant like many, running from the earthquake in her mind. It tells her to run for dear life and never look back on that small Ohio town. There is something disturbingly wrong with this household. Like her daddy, Penelope throws recklessness and propaganda to the winds of personal growth. A tiny body that once walked toward truth has been abducted by the pull of bigotry, sexism, feminism, and blind eyes. But still, I believe in you, Penelope.

Today, a woman stands before you as a reflection of her zealot father. However, beyond this good girl facade is a soul churning with curiosity. Victory is the tale of the wise, rebelling against foolish traditions created by fearful men. A father will punish the daughter, furthering her anxiety in a limitless world. But still, my dear Penelope, I believe in you and your ability to be free.

Daddy's hands were devilish and magnetic, reeling her in by loosened heart strings. He put her to sleep with affirmations of conformity. It was always the same footsteps after midnight, followed by light peeking through her bedroom door. My sweet Penelope, I've known many like you who hide in plain sight. She flinched in terror as daddy's sweaty hands caressed her inner thigh.

I once loved someone who was incapable of escaping a nightmare. The burden was much too heavy for my weakened back to carry. While making love, her trembling body could crumble monuments. His hands were big enough to cover her screams, as mine were also while pleasuring her in her parents' bed. Like you, she also suffered in that partial light every time her bedroom door cracked. Trauma followed her into our bedroom and destroyed our bond.

I constantly chased broken people as a means to settle the nervous uncertainty of my own personal freedom. Thinking it was a birthright to all, I grew enraged when my lover wouldn't free herself from the programming of her father. I searched for that same freedom for myself in others. This was my setback and saving grace at the same time, because I learned that I couldn't control anyone but myself.

Today let freedom ring loudly, causing blood to trickle from the trumpets of destruction. Open your fearful eye to what you thought was an inescapable darkness. You must rebel against the zealot who held onto your fear inside his black heart. You are not his dreams, beliefs, and outdated traditions. Penelope, you are divinely inspired and the highest order amongst celestial beings setting the night ablaze.

You can have the life you've always dreamed of if only you hold onto bravery. However, we must first want it and muster the strength to explore the dark holes of the universe. You've known something was wrong for some time now, and redemption is due. Let not another season pass without causing a natural disaster of your old compliant self. Penelope, I believe in you.

Are you or do you know someone like Penelope?

1. Rebellion is a personal savior when dealing with your programmer's manipulation tactics. Rebel and take flight toward your wildest dreams. Live on your own terms unapologetically.

2. When a parent withdraws love due to personal decisions you make it can potentially crush you. However, it's your life, and this is your path, not theirs.

3. Do you really want to be a reflection of someone else or your own person? Take the good you learned from your parent(s), and let negative attributes that go against your heart die swiftly.

4. Your programmers are not perfect. Like you, they have their own personal demons and compulsions. Remove them from this pedestal they've been placed on by your past self. Begin to see any passed down traits that do not align with your soul's urge. It is up to you to pinpoint the things that were instilled in you that do not represent truth.

Procrastination and How Time Exposes Us

My Friend,

Many of us are free to run as far as the body will take us. We are not confined behind metal bars. We do not wake up atop of concrete floors. There is a different prison where we have dwelled. We have run toward blue skies and made our intentions clear under rainbows. However, our uselessness overshadowed preparations, and we got nowhere.

Now we sit with our eyes to the ground in embarrassment. The great exposing that is time has revealed itself. Time has exposed our tendency to procrastinate and put a cosmic mirror up to a disillusioned ego. We thought of ourselves as safe and untouchable. Time quickly opens our closed eyes to the reality that is life.

The great exposing that is time can be brutally honest with each passing season. We have taken its essence for granted by cheating it with all talk. We didn't move on with time in our back pockets. Instead we ignored time as if it was a threat to our egos. Ignoring the breath only familiarized us with death. Do not walk in death, my friend, but instead run with time. Acknowledge each breath you gasp for as your heartbeat increases. Cherish this marathon and detach yourself from temporary defeats.

Respect your time, and fall in its good graces. Save yourself the embarrassment from time exposing you. In this moment you can come out of your prison. It is in this very moment where you can begin to expose yourself and slay hidden demons.

Cheat time by practicing obedience, routine, and flexibility. Embrace the dark hours, and be unmovable in nights of temporary defeat. Cherish time by adhering to the uncomfortable truth it reveals to you. There is a lesson to be learned in that uncomfortable feeling of being exposed. We only get so many lessons from time until it no longer is present.

The seasons will surely change, but will you? One day the echo of time will become more faint as you grow old. Your time will one day be over, so do not delay in living an authentic life. I am here and willing to listen to you in your darkest hour. Let us find the strength to do today what tomorrow will thank us for.

1. Nothing lasts forever, but regrets can often feel like an eternity. Invest in the currency of time. Yield results that are a direct outcome of following all that is true. I believe in you.

2. Fill your time up with things that will benefit your future self.

3. Share your time with people who respect it and make you forget how fast it goes by.

4. From time to time you will feel lost. You must not stay complacent in this uncertainty. Move as swiftly as the hands on your clock.

5. When time works against you, push back with a stoicism, truth, and adaptability. Be unfazed in pursuit of what you seek.

Conclusion

I hope you find peace in this mad world. Keep shining your light for those in dark corners to see and benefit from. There is greatness within your undying will to live. Thank you for reading these messages. I have a feeling we will be speaking again very soon.

All best,
Your Higher Self

Made in the USA
Monee, IL
29 January 2021

59087741R00066